Facing Autism

✦

A Parent's Guide to a Difficult Journey

Kathleen Mueller

iUniverse, Inc.
New York   Bloomington

Facing Autism

A Parent's Guide to a Difficult Journey

iUniverse books may be ordered through booksellers or by contacting:

iUniverse
1663 Liberty Drive
Bloomington, IN 47403
www.iuniverse.com
1-800-Authors (1-800-288-4677)

ISBN: 978-0-595-48698-4 (pbk)
ISBN: 978-0-595-60795-2 (ebk)

Printed in the United States of America

To Joshua, my darling little boy whom I love so much.
You are the joy in my life and the shining light of my day. You have made me so much stronger than I ever thought possible; I am a better mother because of you. You are my world, and I thank you for everything you have given me.

Contents

Preface: My Story

For years, people encouraged me to write a book about what my husband and I have gone through in raising a child with autism. I didn't want to write a book about myself or even about my son. What I did really want to do, however, was to help other parents who have just learned their children are autistic.

I have spent years looking for and contacting support groups and government agencies to find assistance programs for our son. That's not to mention doctors, therapists, teachers, and school officials. This has entailed hundreds if not thousands of hours researching, e-mailing, calling, and writing. Through this book, I can share the information I have gained through my experience over the years to help other parents learn how to take control of their children's futures, whether through teaching, becoming public advocates, or just being a child's voice when he or she needs it most.

When my son was diagnosed with autism, I didn't know what it was or what to do about it. I wasn't aware of the resources available to me. I didn't know who I needed to contact. The most startling fact, however, was that neither did the professionals who diagnosed him. The diagnosis was fairly new to the physicians in our area at that time. They, too, were just learning what autism was and how to treat it. They gave us a few contact names but had very little information as to what we, as parents, needed to do. Now, several years later, the autism epidemic has spread through the country, but there is still no definitive cause or cure.

MY EXPERIENCE

In an effort to educate myself about autism, I have not only spent hours upon end making contacts with those who could help and give us information; I have also been an active participant in lectures and workshops, both as an attendee and as a speaker.

In 2003, Marbeth Dougherty, a licensed marriage and family therapist and I attended a lecture by Peter E. Tanguay, MD, who is the professor emeritus of child and adolescent psychiatry at the University of Louisville and an expert in autism. Over the years, I have continued to consult with Marbeth Dougherty about my son's progress and about any new information she may receive as a professional.

In 2003, the Wisconsin Parents Association (WPA) asked me to do a workshop at the state's annual homeschooling conference in May. I didn't know if I would have anything to offer, but I knew parents needed support, to know they were not alone in their struggles. Since then, I have taught both workshops and held discussions at the homeschooling conference, both on autism and children with disabilities, and at the time this book was printed, I have been scheduled to teach two more.

Coming together with other parents at these workshops has taught me valuable lessons and given me the chance to share some of those lessons with others. Meeting new parents and their children at these conferences year after year has taught me that many of us share the same struggles and that autism does not discriminate: families of every race, religion, and economic background have been affected by autism.

And yet, despite our differences, one consistent thread runs through all of our stories: autism has turned our lives upside down. Unfortunately, millions of us have that story. In fact, at different points during this book, you may say to yourself, "Hey, that's my story."

Although some of the finer details may differ, the ending is always the same: We have a child with autism and neither our lives nor theirs will ever be the same after we learn the diagnosis. We love them with all our hearts and we want the very best for them. They make our lives richer just by being in them. And although we may not see it at first, with all the struggles we face each day, the reality is that we only become stronger.

THE BABY AND TODDLER YEARS

It all began in 1994, when I married my husband on a hot August day. Our lives were perfect, and like most newlyweds, we wanted to have a baby. Despite our valiant efforts as newlyweds to conceive, however, we had a year with no luck. Then, several months later, on a cold January day, I jumped for joy in my kitchen as I held a positive pregnancy test.

Nine months later the baby arrived, weighing in at nine pounds, ten ounces. He was a perfect little boy who was alert and active. The next several months, we enjoyed our time together as a new family. Like most parents, we dealt with the dirty diapers and the 2 AM feedings with tired but happy faces. Our son continued to grow and meet all milestones on or before the appropriate times. His easygoing personality was shining through with smiles and giggles. He brought joy to our lives.

Around eighteen months old, however, our son began to change. He didn't smile anymore, and he wouldn't laugh. He didn't want to be hugged or touched. He no longer got an attitude when he didn't get his way. He just sat on the floor, rocking back and forth, and moaning. Rather suddenly, our son disappeared. It was as if someone had taken him away and replaced him with a stranger: a distant, unresponsive little boy that lacked everything we had grown to love about him.

All outward signs of communication had vanished. He would now scream when he woke up from a nap instead of saying, "Mama." He no longer smiled when his father came home from work or called out "Dada" when his father walked into the room. Our little boy was gone, and we didn't know how to get him back.

Shortly after we started noticing changes, family and friends began noticing. Some asked why he wasn't talking and smiling as he had before. Some said, "Oh, he's just a boy. They always talk later then girls." I was willing to accept that. I had married into a family of big burly farmers, and they weren't exactly the talking type. But my gut told me something was wrong. I just wasn't willing to admit it to myself yet.

Finally, family convinced me to have him seen by a specialist. He saw many doctors in just a few weeks' time. They tested him for seizures along with blood, urine, hearing, and reflexes, but the results were all within normal range. When they tested his cognitive ability and his physical and social skills, they found he lacked many of the verbal and social skills appropriate for a two-year-old. Finally, the doctors told us that our beautiful little boy whom we loved so much had autism.

Our lives were turned upside down. We didn't know what autism was or what it meant for our son. Doctors often contradicted one another in their recommendations for the best course of action. We were told to put him into an autism therapy group, but first he had to pass five IQ tests. These tests were not covered by our insurance so we were expected to pay over $1,000 to have them administered, which was not a small price to pay in 1998. Our son was two at the time, which meant he wasn't old enough to take three of the five tests. However, the therapists insisted he needed to take them. After the testing was done, they wanted to place him in the therapy group to do a type of therapy called behavioral modification. In an office fifty miles from where we lived, what modification could they do with a two-year-old that couldn't be done at home? So we decided against putting him into the therapy group at that time.

Instead, we took our son to see a doctor who used the drug Secretin in children with autism. (Learn more about Secretin in the chapter titled "Alternative Treatments.") This man ridiculed us for not doing something with our son sooner than we had, and when we asked him questions, we received no answers. Instead, he promptly held up the book he had written and said, "It's in the book." So the only way for us to get answers was to buy his book for $25. We bought it and read it cover to cover. The only thing we learned was that this doctor was just mainly interested in trying to sell his book. The funny but sad thing about this whole situation was that this doctor was recommended by the hospital and the professionals who diagnosed our son with autism. While I'm sure the doctor was trying to do his best, as a parent desperate to find answers about her son, this experience was very frustrating.

Our son was now two-and-a-half, so we still had time to enroll him in the local birth-to-three program in our county. (At the age of three, he would no longer be eligible.) The objective of this county-run program was to help our son meet all those baby milestones he had yet to reach. They worked on fine and gross motor skills, along with speech. Although they had very little success, they did try and were compassionate in dealing with the many obstacles they faced.

At the same time, we began in-home therapy. This particular In-home therapy was not the right choice for our son either, as we had very negative results.

Within six months, we fired that therapy team and hired another. The new team seemed to be the right fit for our son at first, but after about a year, the quality of care and therapy dropped, no longer providing the necessary skills and tools our son needed. So we fired that team, too, and began providing our own therapy.

PRESCHOOL

When our son was three, we enrolled him in the Early Childhood program through the local public school, and had an IEP (Individualized Education Program) written up. He lacked speech skills as well as fine and gross motor skills. He had no attention span and was not toilet-trained. He required constant one-on-one care, and although by law he could not be denied an aide, we had to fight tooth and nail for an aide to accompany him at all times.

At one point before we started therapy and school, he was talking and toilet-training with great success. But then during his first year in the Early Childhood program, our son did not progress. In fact, he regressed, turning inward and withdrawing from the world further. I had known that dealing with autism was new to the school and proved challenging for the teachers and therapists, but something else was not right.

Our son soon started becoming hysterical when it was time to leave for school in the morning. Something in my gut told me there was more going on in the classroom than what I was being told. So I began staying at school during the day, quietly sitting outside the room, listening and occasionally peeking through the window in the door whenever I heard a commotion. What I saw was that there was little if any control over the class. Often, the children were left unsupervised instead of being engaged in structured activities; all the while, the teacher and the aides sat around talking about personal problems.

After noticing that I was observing the teachers and class room from a discreet vantage point; I was invited to attend one of my son's occupational therapy sessions with the schools therapist. During the visit I believe I found the reason for my son's hysterical behavior. During my son's session he was asked to remove his shoes before playing on the many slides and swings available to him in the therapy room. However, the therapist would not show him how to take off his shoes; insisting instead that she showed him how to do so two days prior to this visit. My son spent the entire 20 minutes crying, sitting in a chair looking at all the slides and swings he wasn't allowed to play with. He was being punished for being autistic. The therapist refused to listen to my advice on how my son needed to be taught, and how she needed to show him to take off his shoes. After that visit I insisted my son not attend any more therapy sessions with the school therapists.

Another frustration point was that, from time to time throughout the year, I would meet with the teachers, aides, therapists, and director of Special Education to discuss whether changes should be made to the IEP. At every meeting, without fail, the director threatened to remove my son's aide. I, of course, refused to have my son in school without an aide. I felt I was getting very little help or support. And I was frustrated by feeling that I had to defend my child against the very people who were supposed to be helping him.

The next school year wasn't much better. The year started off with the director of Special Education denying my son an aide. Fortunately, our in-home therapy group offered to send a therapist with him to school in place of an aide. The designated therapist accompanied him to school for the first half of the year, but problems only continued. The therapist reported that our son was being ignored by the teacher and therapists, who were making no effort to teach him or involve him in structured activities. The in-home therapist did her best under the circumstances, having very little say-so in the classroom, which amounted to her basically babysitting my son until class was over.

So at the next IEP meeting, at the end of the first semester, my husband and I decided to take our son out of the Early Childhood classes and keep him home, doing in-home therapy. His therapist at the time was wonderful, and our son liked her very much.

For the next year, however, we were plagued with pressure from the therapy group to increase their hours and have other therapists come to our home. We live in a very rural area over an hour away from the therapy group; most therapists had to drive quite a ways for just a couple hours' work and most didn't want to do that without making more money. Therapists who were assigned to my son's case would attend an average of 4 therapy sessions before requesting to be placed in a home closer to the main office. Most asked to be reassigned, however for those who chose to stay the resentment began to show in the therapists' work. They no longer followed the plan of treatment set up for our son; instead they just babysat him until the time was up.

Therapists also started coming when we didn't want them to. In particular, they started coming at a period during the day that I had set up as "me time." During "me time," I took no phone calls, we did no therapy; my son and I just had quiet time by ourselves. I communicated this clearly with the therapy group, but they refused to accept that I needed time just for me, insisting I could take personal time whenever the therapist was there. However, when she was there, I felt it was important for me to participate, either learning about the therapy or doing it myself.

In addition, the doctor who ran the therapy group, a child psychiatrist, would visit the house every couple of months and observe our son for about thirty minutes each time. As I watched my son decline—becoming less responsive but more aggressive—I began to ask the psychiatrist during these visits if my son had anything else that would account for his increasingly erratic behavior. He gave me the same answer each time—that my son had no other diagnoses, and that he was just autistic and very aggressive. I wasn't satisfied with that answer. And I was not satisfied with the form of therapy being provided by his team of therapists.

Finally my son, at age five, had regressed to the point that he made no sounds at all. No more babbling, no more making syllables or consonant sounds, no more using sign language or picture cards. He no longer communicated in any way. So my husband and I fired the doctor and therapists, and began doing therapy our way and by ourselves. I incorporated my own personal twist into the effective techniques the therapists had taught me, so that the techniques suited my child's direct needs. Within a month, our son started making sounds again, communicating with pictures and gestures. This gave us hope that we had made the right decision.

In reality, every child with autism is unique in what he or she requires as far as therapy, sensory tools, learning approaches, and communication methods. Every child needs a program designed specifically for his or her needs—not a textbook definition of what someone else thinks might work.

That summer, I faced a new obstacle. I no longer had someone to watch my son while I did the grocery shopping. Relatives and friends who previously took care of him during these times began to feel that our son's erratic behavior was worsening, to the point that they could no longer take care of him. So I had to find another way.

While most parents just go grocery shopping, children in tow, that was not a realistic option for us. Because while our son loved to ride in the car, as soon as we pulled into a parking lot, he would start to scream. So I had to condition him to come to the grocery store with me, which proved to be a difficult three-month process.

The first step was to drive him to the store every day, where we would sit in the parking lot until I could talk him into keeping calm. Once he was calm, we would drive home. After several days, once we reached a point where it no longer bothered him to sit in the parking lot, the next step was to take several more trips to town, park, and then get out of the car and walk to the door of the store. When our son could handle that step without screaming, we took the next step of walking him to the door and then stepping inside to let him experience the lights, sounds, and sights of the store, which can be very overwhelming for a child with autism. Then we walked back out to the car and went home. We continued this pattern for about three months until he was able to walk all the way through the store without screaming.

Eventually we were able to shop together on most days. At times when we weren't able to, I had to toss this kicking, screaming five-year-old boy over my shoulder, because I could no longer carry him in my arms. (Our son was always a big guy. At five years old, he weighed sixty-five pounds and stood over four feet tall. He was getting to the point that picking him up in any way was a challenge, but adding a full-blown tantrum in a store of glaring people to the mix, and the task of lifting him was nearly impossible.) During these tantrums, we would have no choice but to walk out, leaving our cart of groceries for someone else to put away.

Perhaps those outings wouldn't have been so difficult if some fellow parents had offered their support. Instead, people just watched and made rude remarks. In fact, the nasty comments some people made were more difficult than the tantrums themselves. And often, unfortunately, the older the spectator, the more intolerant.

During this three-month period, I helped my son acclimate to the stores during the day, and then I went shopping at night. I would have to wait for my husband to get home to watch our son and often would not return home from shopping until close to midnight.

By fall, however, our son had progressed in his social awareness enough that his being in stores or other public places no longer caused immediate tantrums. We had finally made some progress.

The School Years

Finally, the time came for public school. After our bad experiences with the school district's Early Childhood program, however, we decided to enroll him in another school district. (In our state, open enrollment is available to qualified children.)

The new school district's director of Special Education was wonderful. He set up a meeting with a team of teachers and therapists who would be involved with our son's education. I was very optimistic, hoping we had found a school right for our son. After the meeting, however, the director and therapists were honest enough to tell us they were not equipped to handle a child with his degree of disability. I was thankful for the up-front attitude but now faced another obstacle. Where did we go from here?

The director of Special Education suggested homeschooling our son. I knew next to nothing about homeschooling, but I did know a friend of the family who homeschooled her children. So that's were I started. I asked lots of questions and, fortunately, received lots of answers and support.

By fall, our son had started his first year in a homeschool environment. I learned that the constant one-on-one attention that came with homeschooling was not only essential to his learning but also the key to opening up his ability to communicate. By January, he began to say small one-syllable words. He also continued spelling words using plastic letters, an ability that we had discovered he had when he was three years old. We were amazed at the knowledge hidden behind those distant, unresponsive eyes; we learned that, without a doubt, a diagnosis of autism is not a diagnosis of lack of intelligence. Quite the contrary—our son was very intelligent. It was *we* who had to learn how to communicate with *him*. The more we opened up those lines of communication, the more our son learned and the more we learned about him. The results confirmed that our homeschooling our son was the right choice.

That's not to say that everything was suddenly perfect, however. In the following months, our son's tantrums started to become extremely violent. His behavior was so unpredictable that we never knew what would set him off. For years, my husband and I had asked doctors whether our son might have any disorders or diseases besides autism. Other children I met with autism were not as aggressive as our son. During his outbreaks, he would smash windows and bust holes the size of basketballs in the walls. He would pick up anything he could get his hands on, throwing it as hard as he could at us or at the wall. Several times, he bit me hard enough to draw blood or scratched me so deep that I still have scars there today. I was physically black and blue from the hitting, kicking, and headbutting. He would also have bruises on him; most of them were from banging his head into the wall. I was sure there had to be more going on than autism.

It was then we decided to take him to another child psychiatrist, who almost immediately diagnosed him with depression and, about a year later, with bipolar disorder. He was put on medication for both. Within a week of being treated for bipolar disorder, the violent mood swings stopped. To this day, they have not returned. Now, we must treat my son daily for autism, depression, bipolar disorder, and allergies. Unfortunately, without those many medications he would be out of control. But, we know without a doubt that these medications, when maintained at a therapeutic level, are helping. He is not drugged into a stoned mummy-like state. Instead, he becomes very alert and active. His attention span increases greatly, speech is much clearer, he is calm and focused, and his communication skills continue to increase. These positive affects are extremely evident when he has the flu and can't hold any medication down; without fail, the negative behaviors start to return.

For a while, we struggled with one major side affect of most of our son's medications: weight gain. All of his periods of major weight gain corresponded to introducing a medication or increasing a current dosage, and he was already a large child, in the ninety-fifth percentile for height and weight from the time he was a baby. The only solution, however, would have been to take him off of the medication, which would mean dealing with violent mood swings from a child who was now over five foot tall and outweighed his mother.

So we took our concerns to our doctor who referred us to an Endocrinologist. He ran many tests relating to hormone imbalances, and thyroid conditions, along with blood work to check for high cholesterol, elevated sugar levels, and high triglycerides. The doctor's concluded our son was perfectly healthy with no outstanding health issues other then the one's he was currently being treated for. The Doctor said our son's weight gain was a direct result of the medications he took. And as long as we kept him on a healthy diet, stayed active and monitored his blood levels throughout the year he should be just fine.

So we decided to deal with the weight gain and be satisfied just knowing our son was happy. We knew without a doubt that the medication helped him. It helped him to communicate his many moods with words, gestures, and facial expressions. It brought out his easygoing nature, which we hadn't seen since he'd been a baby. It left him in high spirits and enabled him to show affection to those closest to him. Now, we can even see him laugh at jokes; slapstick comedy seems to be his favorite. And he pretends—every day, he acts like he's a different character and often engages others in his imaginative play.

So while being off of the medication may have kept him thin, it would have also left him miserable, unhappy, and frustrated, unable to understand or express his erratic emotions.

One of the realities of being a parent of an autistic child, however, is that no matter how clear it was to us that medication was the best choice for our son, it was still a choice that we struggled with. We still worried about the health risks involved with our child being overweight. And we still worry, even to this day.

ACCEPTING OUR SON AND WHAT THE FUTURE MIGHT BE

We love the special uniqueness of our son's personality. He loves to laugh. Often, he will do things to make other people laugh and then tell us he is being silly. Or, while watching a movie, he bursts out laughing at some remark or stunt that tickles his funny bone. However delightful our son is, we don't know what the future holds for him.

Likewise, many parents of children with autism are faced with such a reality: that their child may never be "normal" again and will always require special care. Although some children are only slightly affected and recover quite well, others suffer severely and require intensive care. (In fact, this wide range of severity is why autism is called a *spectrum* disorder.) So until we find the true cause of autism, not to mention its cure, for children whose cases are severe, the future is uncertain. And this uncertainty can create a sense of hopelessness—unless you make a decision to remember and focus on the good things.

We focus on the reality that regardless of the future, our son makes us truly happy. He brings joy into our lives. We are thankful for his beautiful, smiling face that lights up each day. We take pleasure in the simple moments: his dad has fun playing pirate or Darth Vader with him, engaging in plastic sword fights. I get excited when he learns fractions while we bake cookies together. His dad and I are encouraged when we see him do chores, gladly helping to put away groceries, empty the dishwasher, vacuum his room, or water and collect eggs from our chickens.

He loves many things, and we love to watch him enjoy life: sitting in our bed during reading class, pointing out the words as we read together; riding the tractor with Dad, who sometimes lets him drive while he sits next to him, guiding his turns; visiting his cousins, aunts, and uncles at their farms, riding their horses or watching the cows. I remember a wonderful trip to Grandma's and Grandpa's farm to see newborn calves. And he loves to visit his other grandparents in Tennessee—Grandpa gives him peanut-butter bars and Grandma gives him rides in her truck. Because our son is who he is, we receive enjoyment from seeing his positive reactions to experiences, such enjoyment that we are convinced our lives are better for it.

Through all of this, we have learned to enjoy his uniqueness, and we have realized that his quirkiness is what makes him special. We have also come to an acceptance of the fact that our child will always be different. And as parents of autistic children, finding that acceptance, acceptance in who they are and in what their futures hold, is one of the greatest gifts we can give them.

What Is Autism and How Is It Diagnosed?

THE HISTORY OF AUTISM

Eugene Bleuler, a Swiss psychiatrist first coined the term *autism* in 1911. At that time, however, the term was associated with adult schizophrenia.

In fact, it wasn't until well into the late 1960s that people began to understand autism and more precisely identify its symptoms and treatments as separate from those of schizophrenia.[1] As part of this emerging awareness, Bernard Rimland, PhD, founded the Autism Society of America (ASA) in 1965. Today, the ASA is a community of over 120,000 members offering help, support, and public awareness.[2]

In addition, there are now specific criteria for diagnosing autism, which means many more medical professionals are specifically equipped to make a diagnosis. And with autism becoming an epidemic nationwide, treatment is now available in every state.

---

[1] Autism and Pdd Support Network. What is Autism? "The History of Autism." http://www.autism-pdd.net
[2] Autism Society of America. History page. http://www.autism-society.org

WHAT IS AUTISM?

The Columbia Encyclopedia[3] says that autism is a neurological disorder that affects the brain, causing developmental disability. The main characteristic of the disorder is the abnormal development of communication skills. Although autistic children may appear normal until around thirty months, some parents may know or suspect autism as early as birth, while others may not know until long after thirty months.

WHAT ARE THE SYMPTOMS?

Children who have autism will display the following symptoms of autism, which can vary widely in severity:

- They show a lack of eye-to-eye contact
- They often repeat words or phrases
- They have abrupt and unexplained outbursts
- They lack age-appropriate ability to express thoughts and feelings
- They show insensitivity to physical pain.[4]

If you suspect that your child is autistic, make a list of the symptoms you've noticed, with specific circumstances relating to each symptom, and take it with you to the doctor. (A checklist has been provided later in the chapter.) With a list right in front of you, you're less likely to forget mentioning something important, the result being a more timely and accurate diagnosis of your child.[5]

WHAT ARE THE CAUSES?

The topic of what causes autism fuels anger in a lot of parents, but the exact cause still remains unclear. Along with that, the question as to way so many of our children are being diagnosed autistic remains unclear.

Neurological studies have been done on brain dysfunction, genetic disorders, diet and food sensitivity, and heavy-metal buildup, and yet the search continues.

---

[3] Autism and Pdd Support Network. What is Autism? "Autism—Definition from *Columbia Encyclopedia*." http://www.autism-pdd.net
[4] ————. "Autism Symptoms." http://www.autism-pdd.net
[5] ————. "Autism Symptom Checklist." http://www.autism-pdd.net

As of January 2008, scientists at the University of California-Davis found eleven genes governing what they call "natural killer" immune cells. These cells are more active in autistic children than in nonautistic children. Although the study is small, it supports theories that something infectious was introduced to affected children early in life, and it provides hope that scientists will soon be able to find markers for preventing autism as well as create effective treatments.[6]

In addition, scientists are trying to determine the reason for the rapid rise in autism diagnoses in recent years. Many people, including some medical professionals, believe that Thimerosol, a preservative containing mercury is the culprit.[7] The amount of Thimerosol that has been routinely used in childhood vaccines since the 1930s can be toxic to the human body. The number of childhood vaccines has risen dramatically, resulting in children being exposed too much higher doses of toxic heavy metals than in the past. Although most but not all childhood vaccines, today have had the Thimerosol reduced or removed, some still contain the preservative. However, neither the parents nor the doctors know which vaccines are free of Thimerosol and which are not. That information about which vaccines are Thimerosol-free has not been released, to the medical community or its patients.[8] To learn more about mercury poisoning, go to http://www.healthsentinel.com. In addition, the number of childhood vaccines being administered has risen dramatically in recent years, resulting in the risk of more exposure to toxic heavy metals than ever before.[9]

As the number of families affected by autism grows, so must our awareness and our desire to find the cure. We must work together in this fight for the future of our children.

DIAGNOSING AUTISM

The Diagnostic and Statistical Manual of Mental Disorders, otherwise known as the DSM, is the manual used by medical- and mental-healthcare professionals to help diagnose and describe mental disorders. The manual contains lists of characteristics for various mental disorders, including autism.

---

[6] Carrie Peyton Dahlberg, "Genes Linked to Autism Found." *Wisconsin State Journal.* 1/26/2008 A3

[7] To learn more about mercury poisoning, go to http://www.healthsentinel.com.

[8] Centers for Disease Control and Prevention. Vaccine Safety. "Mercury and Vaccines (Thimerosol)." http://www.cdc.gov/vaccinesafety/concerns/thimerosal.htm

[9] Autism and Pdd Support Network: What Is Autism? "What Causes Autism?" http://www. autism-pdd.net

When a healthcare professional finds specified number of those characteristics is present in ranges inappropriate for a child's age, autism is diagnosed.

Autism diagnoses usually occur in patients between the ages of three and five, but improvement among individual autism patients varies. A broad range of studies have come to similar conclusions about the overall rate of improvement, however, with about 2 percent of all patients attaining normal functioning and 40 percent improving to a level called high-functioning autistic, a condition otherwise known as Asperger's Syndrome.[10]

What to Look for in Baby Development

The following chart notes the *average* progress of children from zero to four years old in terms of communication milestones. Keep in mind, however, that the vast majority of children who do not meet these milestones still end up with normal language skills, because not all children progress at the same rate; so while other babies may be more advanced than your child in some of these areas, your child will likely surpass them in others.

Baby's Communication Milestones	Average Age
Smiles socially	0–2 Months
Coos	0–3 Months
Turns toward parent's voice	4 Months
Makes razzing sounds	5 Months
Recognizes parent or caregiver	6–9 Months
Says first word	12 Months
Has vocabulary of 8 to10 words	18 Months
Speaks in 2-word phrases; has a vocabulary of 50 words	20–24 Months
Can answer who, why, and where questions	3 Years
Has a vocabulary of 500 words and can tell a story	4 Years

Taken from the Autism and Pdd Support Network Web site, http://www.autism-pdd.net

A good way to evaluate your child is to keep a Baby Book recording all of the milestones and changes your baby goes through and noting the date and the age your baby was at the time of each. Writing these special moments

---

[10]Autism and Pdd Support Network. "Diagnosing Autism." http://www.autism-pdd.net

down will be a great help to your doctor in diagnosing any developmental delays.

A bonus of the Baby Book: it's wonderful to look back and see the changes that happened in your baby's first few years. Babies change so quickly, and with life passing by so quickly, it's nice to have something to remind us of when they were tiny bundles that fit comfortably in our arms.

A Personal Checklist: Criteria to Diagnose Autism

You and your doctor should use similar criteria to determine whether a diagnosis of autism is in order for your child. The following checklist, derived from criteria in the fourth edition of the DSM, could be a good place to start.[11] Simply check the items that you feel apply to your child and take this with you to your child's doctor appointment.

Your child shows impairment in many nonverbal behaviors, including the following:

___A. Does not make direct eye contact.

___B. Has limited or no facial expressions.

___C. Lacks correct body posture.

___D. Does not use gestures such as pointing and waving.

___E. Fails to make friends with peers.

___F. Lacks desire to seek enjoyment, interests, or achievements with others.

___G. Does not actively join in simple social games.

___H. Prefers being alone.

___I. Uses others as tools or mechanical aides during activities.

---

[11] Autism and Pdd Support Network. "Diagnosing Autism." DSM-IV criteria from the Diagnostic and Statistical Manual of Mental Disorders, 4th Edition, 1994. http://www.autism-pdd.net

Your child shows impaired communication skills, including the following:

___A. Shows a lack of, or a delay in, spoken language.

___B. Lacks the ability to start or participate in a conversation.

___C. Repeats the same words or mimics words.

___D. Cannot play make-believe or imitate others.

___E. Is unable to play at developmental age.

Your child shows repetitive patterns of behavior in both interests and activities, including the following:

___A. Becomes preoccupied with one or more items.

___B. Focuses on certain objects with abnormal intensity.

___C. Throws tantrums when routines or rituals are varied.

___D. Shows repetitive hand, finger, and body movements (e.g., flapping, twisting, rocking).

___E. Shows preoccupation with certain parts of objects (e.g., wheels on toy cars).

If your child shows many of the delays mentioned above in regard to social interaction, social communication, and make-believe play, and if his behaviors cannot be better explained by Rett's Disorder or Childhood Disintegrative Disorder, take your concerns to your doctor as soon as possible. Early intervention is the most effective first step in dealing with autism.

Also know that diagnosing autism and Asperger's Syndrome is a *process*—and a difficult one, especially for young children whose speech and reasoning skills are still developing. It's essential that this process include the assessment and evaluation of a child's development, as well as his communication and social skills.. Then, even after an initial diagnosis is made, it is essential to have a long-term treatment plan that includes ongoing evaluations and assessments: so that in other words, once a diagnosis has been made, this process should be repeated periodically. So adjustments can be made to medications or treatment plans, as needed.

The following tests may help with making a diagnosis or implementing changes in treatment strategies:[12]

MEDICAL TESTING: Tests for hearing; electroencephalogram (EEG) tests, to measure brain waves; metabolic screening (blood and urine tests); Magnetic Resonance Imaging (MRI) to create a detailed image of the brain; Computer-Assisted Axial Tomography scans (CAT SCANs) to take thousands of pictures of the brain; and genetic tests (blood work)

THERAPY EVALUATIONS: Speech-language therapy, occupational therapy, physical therapy

DIRECT OBSERVATION: Interaction and interview assessments, functional assessments, play-based assessments

STANDARDIZED INSTRUMENTS: Rating scales and developmental inventories (e.g., the Vineland Adaptive Behavior Scales, the Childhood Autism Rating Scale); Intelligence Quotient (IQ) tests (e.g., the Stanford-Binet Intelligence Scale, the Wechsler Intelligence Scale for Children, the Verbal IQ [VIQ] test, the Performance IQ [PIQ] test, and the Full-Scale IQ [FSIQ] test).

Many parents are not aware of all the medical testing out there that can help to properly diagnose autism. I did not have this information when we were going through the initial diagnosis process, and I wish I had. I hope this information proves useful for parents whose children are going through the early diagnosis and treatment stages in the same way that it helped me later on in the process.

---

[12] Autism and Pdd Support Network What is Autism? "Autism Symptoms Checklist." http://www.autism-pdd.net

My Child Has Been Diagnosed Autistic—Now What Do I Do?

Receiving a diagnosis of autism can be a time of confusion and uncertainty. Many parents have no idea what to do, where to go, or who to ask for help in dealing with the many challenges they will soon face.

Some doctors and clinics are much more educated about what the next plan of action should be for an autistic child and his family. Some of these physicians even belong to a community that is knowledgeable about dealing with autism and offers support. However, not everyone lives in an area with such a great network.

Regardless of your circumstances, early intervention is key. Taking a proactive role in your child's future will help ensure a happy one.

THERAPY AND EDUCATION

If your child is still young, you may wish to start him in a birth-to-three program usually run by the county or local government. Such a program should provide physical, occupational, and speech therapy to help your child reach those baby milestones that they may be behind in reaching.

You could also hire private therapists to come into your home or do therapy yourself. Another option is to schedule regular therapy sessions at a clinic, with a licensed therapist who is trained to deal with autistic children.

There are several methods of therapy used with autistic children, such as the Lovass Method, the Greenspan Method, and others. Educate yourself on these methods. Find out which method your therapist will use and then, once therapy is in progress, think about whether it is appropriate for your child.

For example, for over three years I used both the Lovass and Greenspan methods with my son and had very negative results. It was not the type of therapy my son needed. However, I know of families who are receiving wonderful results from both the Lovass and Greenspan methods of therapy. Methods should be applied on an individual basis, because what may be good for one child will be a huge mistake for another.

If you are unsure what to do, I recommend trying a therapy group for no more than three months. If you see positive improvements in your child within that time, it is the right fit; if it's not the right fit, your child will regress or not improve at all.

Please understand, however, that you don't need to put your child into therapy to help him get better, but especially for working parents, it is a practical alternative. In today's age, that second paycheck is often crucial, and regardless of what your reasons are for needing to work outside the home, there are very few stay-at-home parents; for the majority of parents, therapy services are essential.

Having a stay-at-home parent can be a blessing for an autistic child. If you are one such parent you may, as mentioned, wish to have in-home therapy for your child or even do your own brand of therapy. There is no right or wrong answer. You may receive pressure from doctors or other professionals who tell you that you can't do this yourself, but don't be intimidated. I did it and so can you. If you have the desire, all you need to do is to educate yourself on the various types of therapy and see which type your child responds to in a positive way.

So much information is constantly available on the Internet, so you can always educate yourself with new techniques such as hands-on learning, sign language, picture cards, and computer software. Patience and imagination have been my greatest tools in teaching my son, and for any parent they will be the largest weapons in your arsenal in fighting autism.

As your child reaches school age you may wonder whether school will be the right fit for your child. The answer often depends on the school. This is a time when some autistic children will regress, and you may need to consider that your child, although academically ready for a public school setting, may not be emotionally ready. You will need to evaluate your child's progress in such a setting and decide whether to keep him home for another year and homeschool him or perhaps enroll him in a different school district. The rules governing the enrollment of a child in another school district vary from state to state and often also from school district to school district. Check with both school districts to see what the protocol is in your area. Your local school district may fight to keep you there, because school districts receive government dollars for the number of children attending their schools. They won't want to loose the government dollars they receive from having your child attend a school in that district.

FAMILY SUPPORT PROGRAMS

Here are some other things you may need to be aware of when you get that diagnosis of autism. Most states have programs such as Family Support, which helps families with autistic children pay for various necessities such as unique materials for learning, special medications not covered by insurance, and even modifications to your home, for example, the addition of essentials such as swings, trampolines, bikes, or bathroom adaptations.

There are also programs that assist autistic children as they grow older. Not all states offer the same type of support or have the same programs. The most important thing you can do right now is to make sure your child's name is on all of the various programs' waiting lists. There are so many children with special needs that, in some cases, waiting lists can be several years long. Most counties will keep track of where your child is on the list and will inform you throughout the year as to any changes in placement.

My son was on the Family Support list for four years before we began receiving services, but I'm so happy I didn't wait. That list is now much longer, which means parents are waiting longer than I did to receive services.

Also know that the funding for young children is different than what's available for teenagers, so sign up on both lists.

DAILY ROUTINES

I found it important to keep a loose routine for my son. Likewise, I know other parents who have said that not allowing change into their routines created more problems, causing their child to act out or have outbursts. But again, what works for one child may not work for another. If you have found that keeping a strict routine with your child helps, then that's what you need to do. Do what works best for you.

I found that breaking up my son's routine with pleasant activities or with something positive taught him to deal with change better. Soon he enjoyed changes in routine, and when something unexpected would happen that wasn't positive, it seems he was able to deal with the situation much better than other special-needs children I have heard about.

For example, Special Education teachers have told me that when they had fire drills, they were always the last ones to exit the school because they'd have to deal with screaming, violent students; the unexpected change in routine caused their special-needs children to have wild outbursts.

The positive affects on my son that resulted from my purposely introducing change to his routine was never more evident than on June 6, 2006. Our farm was destroyed by a tornado. That summer, my son's entire life was thrown into chaos, but he dealt with it by becoming a part of the clean-up process. We gave him jobs to pick up debris, and then later, he helped rebuild structures that had been demolished, literally *working* through the devastation left by the tornado. Had his previous routine been extremely rigid, he may not have dealt with this tragedy as well as he did.

Life is chaos. Nothing in life ever stays the same or responds the same way all the time. Teaching our children to deal with the chaos of life will help them as they grow older. You may even realize that by teaching such lessons of flexibility, you are actually helping your child become more well-adjusted, making your life a little easier in the long run.

On the other hand, this technique may not work for you. Always do what is right for you and what works best for your family—that is what's most important.

Social Support

One thing my husband and I have learned is that it's important to build a support system. Having a group of people whom you trust to help you with all aspects of raising an autistic child is essential. Here are some people who you should consider part of your personal network.

> **Doctors and nurses**. Your child probably sees particular physicians on a regular basis. These "regulars" can help you with the many health issues that face your child. The more they see your child, the more educated and involved they will become in dealing with him, making this relationship important, especially when you need medical advice or referrals to other doctors.

Therapists and teachers. These individuals may spend several hours a day with your child in school and at home. They are important to have in your network, because teachers can communicate with you about your child's progress in school, while in-home therapists can update you about your child's progress during times you are away from home.

Family and friends. Finding people close to you who are willing to watch your child and give you and your spouse some needed time to yourselves is a must-have. Having friends who are also raising a special needs child is helpful. Often you find that you share the same concerns and frustrations in raising your children.

When communicating with others in your social network, it's important to be proactive and to take a hands-on approach to everything in your child's life. Asking questions and finding out details will help you learn how others deal with your child and, if needed, also guide you to be more explicit with the information you offer about his care.

Constant communication with the people in your support system is vital. Providing updates about your child's growth and development, about what upsets him or makes him happy, and about the most recent special therapies or medications that have proven effective will help them better care for your child.

When it comes to school and therapy, we parents need to be constantly informed as to how our child is doing. A great way to communicate about your child is to keep a notebook in his backpack that you and the teacher can write in to each other. That way, if problem behaviors or learning issues arise, you will know about them immediately rather than at the next parent/teacher conference. To do this, begin by choosing a three-ring binder, a special notebook, or a folder with paper for notes in the center. Stop into your child's classroom and discuss the folder with his teacher, therapists, and aides. Let them know you would like daily communication with them as to how your child is doing. On a normal day, a simple remark may be fine, but on days your child is having difficulty, notes can inform both the teacher and parent to be aware of what has already happened that day or what might transpire. An advantage to the notebook: charting your child's day to day progress. Likewise, you will have the benefit of looking back at old notes, noting any patterns or changes in behavior, thus allowing adjustments to be made in his routine or schedule that may be affecting his outbursts or his lack of interest in school. Here are examples of short yet informative notes that can help the parent and teacher communicate.

Date: 1-23-2008

Parent:

Billy had an ear infection over the weekend. He may be a little tired and irritable today. Please call if he needs to go home.

Teacher:

Billy did well until an hour before school ended. He began acting out in class. An aide took him into another room for some quiet time. He was calmer by the time the bus came.

Another simple form of communication, not with teachers but with fellow parents, is an Internet message board or chat room. A wonderful support Web site, http://www.dailystrength.org, provides parents of autistic children with a place to share personal stories and photos. By far the most important thing you will find there, however, is that you are not alone.

In this busy day and age, we need simple ways such as this to communicate about our children when they are in the care of others.

Alternative Treatments

We would all love to wake up one day and hear they've done it: they've found a cure for autism. Our children need only to take one little pill and the autism will disappear. The reality, however, is that we are always searching and hoping to find a new therapy, medication, or procedure that will bring our children back to us and out of the world of autism.

This search can be a lot of work, not to mention confusing. So many different treatments and therapies are available to parents of autistic and disabled children today that we sometimes don't know the good from the bad. Some of these therapies have been abandoned, while others continue to show some success.

The following treatments have been used in treating Autism Spectrum Disorders with various degrees of success. (Please note: Always speak to your personal physician before starting any alternative treatments.)

THE DAN! PROTOCOL

Defeat Autism Now (DAN) was founded by Dr. Bernard Rimland in the 1960s as a way to train doctors in the DAN! Protocol. DAN doctors believe that autism is a biomedical disorder caused by a lowered immune response, external toxins from vaccines and other sources, and allergic responses to certain foods. DAN doctors will test your child for food allergies and treat intestinal bacterial/yeast overgrowth by implementing special diets.[13] They

---

[13] Lisa Jo Rudy, "About the Autism Research and the DAN Protocol." Biomedical Treatments for Autism. http://www.autism.about.com/od/treatmentoptions/a/DANQandA.htm

will also add supplements, vitamins, minerals, amino acids, and fatty acids to the diet. Doctors can also detoxify the body of heavy metals through Chelation Therapy. (Although, please note that Chelation Therapy has been known to cause death in some cases.) You can go to http://www.about.com to learn the pros and cons of using the DAN! Protocol.

NATIVE REMEDIES

For centuries the Native American people lived off the land successfully, healing their people using herbs, roots, and other natural substances. Passing along the knowledge of healing from one generation to the next was a Native tradition. Many of the foods, vitamins, and medications we take today are no longer made from natural substances. Instead, they are synthetic, made by a scientist in a laboratory, and are often filled with inactive ingredients such as wax and starch along with other substances most of us can't even pronounce.

If you would like to learn more about Native remedies, http://www.manataka.org is a Web site with natural treatments for autism, depression, ADHD, mood swings, repetitive behaviors, aggression, and anxiety. The site offers remedies in the form of drops for children and in the appropriate dosage amounts for adults.[14]

SECRETIN

Secretin is a hormone involved in the regulation of gastric functions. It is administered by IV injection to increase the water and bicarbonate in the pancreas. There has been a lot of controversy regarding the effectiveness and safety of this medication being prescribed off-label. Although very few studies have been conducted to support the theory that Secretin helps with autism, many have experienced positive results. More information is available at http://www.osiris.sunderland.ac.uk/autism/sec.[15]

CRANIOSACRAL THERAPY

---

[14] Manataka American Indian Council. Native Remedies. "Proven Natural Treatment for Autistic Children, Teens, and Adults." http://www.manataka.org/page904.html

[15] Autism Research Unit. "The Use of Secretin for the Treatment of Autism." http://www.osiris.sunderland.ac.uk/autism/sec.htm

CranioSacral Therapy began in the twentieth century with Dr. William Sutherland's development of a method known as Cranial Osteopathy. CranioSacral Therapy uses touch to help balance the membranes and tissues neighboring the spine and brain, called cerebrospinal fluid. Parents have reported their children seeming more relaxed, showing more signs of communication, and having better eye contact after receiving CranioSacral Therapy. Speak to a licensed therapist if you wish to learn more about CranioSacral Therapy or want to have it done on your child. To learn more, try this Web site: http://www.healing-arts.org.[16]

HYPERBARIC OXYGEN TREATMENT

Hyperbaric oxygen is natural oxygen that has been found to be helpful for autoimmune disorders. For treatment, a child sits in a pressurized chamber that has twice the normal air pressure and ten times the regular amount of oxygen. The body inhales 2.4 pounds of oxygen in one hour, causing the red blood cells to fill with oxygen. As a result, tissue oxygen levels rise far above normal. This treatment method has been scientifically proven to stimulate healing, but treatment must occur as early as possible before any irreversible damage is sustained. Find more detailed information at http://www.healing-arts.org.[17]

LIVE CELL AND STEM CELL THERAPY

Dr. Niehans from Switzerland developed Live Cell Therapy in the 1930s. Patients were cured from a variety of illnesses after receiving injections of live cell extracts from healthy animal organs. It appeared the live cells offered distinctive biochemicals needed by the unhealthy gland or organ but were found to be unattainable elsewhere. Doctors tend to agree in this alternative form of treatment. To read more in-depth about Live Cell and Stem Cell Therapy, go to http://www.healingarts.org.[18]

ANTIFUNGAL TREATMENT

---

[16] Autism Treatments. "CranioSacral Therapy (CST) for Autistic Children." http://www.healing-arts.org/children/craniosacral.htm

[17] ———. "Hyperbaric Oxygen Treatment Study." http://www.healing-arts.org/children/hyperbaric.htm

[18] ———. "Live Cell & Stem Cell Therapy." http://www.healing-arts.org/children/cell.htm

Autistic children often have poor bowel ecology marked by an overgrowth of fungi and other microbes. Autistic children who score high for yeast and anaerobic bacteria are eligible for this type of treatment, because of the belief that an overgrowth of a yeast-like fungus may make autistic symptoms more pronounced. There are a variety of treatments used to treat yeast overgrowth, such as antifungal medications, nutritional supplements, and dietary changes. Antifungal treatment is not known to cure autism, but improvement of health and autistic behaviors have been reported after treatment. A list of medications that doctors prescribe for this kind of treatment and more can be found at http://www.healing-arts.org.[19]

These are just a few of the treatments and therapies available to autistic children today. The key to making your way through the various options is to educate yourselves on any new treatment you might be considering.

Also know that despite our years searching for treatments and therapies that might help our son, at the end of the day we find that the only thing that truly helps is never giving up. Our children need us to keep looking and hoping to find something that will break down that wall they are hiding behind.

---

[19] ———. "Anti-Fungal Treatment." http://www.healing-arts.org/children/anitfungal.htm

Homeschooling and Providing Therapy—Yes You Can!

Homeschooling can be beneficial for children with special needs; however, it is not just something you can jump into. You need to be well prepared and informed about what the process entails. There are many resources available to you that offer the information and knowledge you need not only to get started, but to succeed.

Before you homeschool, the first and most important thing is to know about the related laws in your state. The Web site www.homeschooling. about.com has a listing of those laws for all fifty states, along with parental rights and other related information. It also offers tips on how to get started homeschooling as well as information about parent support groups.

Another good resource is someone you know who already homeschools. Veteran homeschoolers are not only great resources of information but also solid candidates for your personal support system, something that will be essential should you ever need to deal with interference from public school officials (an unfortunate reality, even if only occasionally, as some school systems will try to intimidate parents into keeping their children in public schools).

Once you have a good grasp of the basics, you'll be ready to roll up your sleeves and get your hands dirty. To help you get started, here are some crucial first steps you can take as well as important things to keep in mind:

1. **Spend time learning about your child's abilities.** Watch and listen carefully to your child, so you can learn what his strengths and challenges are. Start by giving him tasks such as drawing a circle, pointing to a picture, or saying a word. Reward him for any attempt he makes and—if he won't move onto something different, like standing up, sitting down, or jumping on one leg— encourage him to try again. Of course, these activities are only examples. Depending on your child's abilities, you may need to make the tasks easier or harder.

2. **Take notes and keep records.** Chart how your child is doing before you decide what type of lessons he needs. He may have varying levels of ability which may differ among different subjects (for example, he may be at a preschool level for math but a third-grade level for reading; or at a first-grade level in history and a second-grade level in science), so what or how you teach him may need to differ from subject to subject. This will help you later when you create a curriculum, as you can adjust it for each subject to fit the varying learning levels he is at, perhaps changing teaching techniques from doing hands-on activities for one subject to doing more traditional table work for another subject.

You'll also want note how well your child attends to a lesson and how long his attention span is during each subject. For example, my son has an advanced reading level but can't write at all. As a result, his attention span during reading class is excellent, but is only five minutes during writing. Knowing all this helps me to tailor a curriculum and teaching style for each subject in a way that he will be most responsive to.

3. **Create a curriculum.** You can purchase a curriculum for a specific grade level that will guide you through what your child should learn for that year, giving you lesson

plans, worksheets, books, and software. You can follow the curriculum strictly or use it to help you create your own specialized one.

A good way to start creating your own is by making an outline of what subjects you want your child to study along with any projects you want him to finish per semester or just by the end of the school year.

Sometimes it is easier to write a basic outline with the main subjects you wish to cover, adding projects to the outline as you go—sometimes projects are born of the most unpredictable things. For example, 2 years ago, Mars and Venus came very close to Earth, so we started a project of looking at the planets and stars through a telescope each night.

4.   **Set goals your child can reach.** Set standards for your child that he alone can meet. Often parents feel inadequate around other parents who seem to have children learning at rates their child has yet to attain or doing things their child has yet to master. But making unrealistic goals for your child to meet will only frustrate both him and you.

Just be proud of what your child can do—and go ahead and brag. If your eight-year-old has just learned to tie his shoes, then you should be very proud he has learned something you taught him. Smile, for you have done well. Enjoy his little triumphs, for they are your triumphs too.

5.   **Take time to do prep work.** Starting class organized will help keep your child's attention focused on the subject at hand. I learned this lesson the hard way. I would start a subject and have my son's full attention, but then when I'd prepare to move onto another subject, I'd have to take a few moments to gather my materials and organize what we were going to do. In that time, my son would become bored waiting for me, and I would lose his wonderful attentiveness.

6.   **Reward your child for the smallest accomplishment.**
Your child will try harder if school is pleasant and
rewarding. Stickers are always fun, but you can be creative
too. Here's an example: when doing speech therapy with
my son, I wanted to encourage him to speak. So even
if he'd said a word incorrectly or so softly that I could
hardly hear him, I would hoot and holler, clapping my
hands with a huge smile on my face. This would get my
son excited, and as a result, he would try hard to say
the next word—so he could see my little show again.
He also learned what a happy face looks like with my
exaggerated smile. Now, many years later, I no longer
need to be so dramatic.

7.   **Begin slowly.** Pushing too hard or too fast may cause
your child to withdraw and regress by making learning
a stressful, negative experience. Sometimes it's easy to
forget that our special-needs children learn differently
from other kids, and we should not expect them to learn
like others. Instead, we should take our time and, while
pushing hard enough to challenge them to move forward,
not push to the point that they become frustrated. Allow
them to learn at their own pace.

8.   **Use tools to transition from one subject to the next.**
For example, in between lessons, offer your child Play-
Doh or crayons and markers for about five minutes. This
will encourage creativity, fine and gross motor skills, and
imagination. A snack or musical instrument can be used
as well. This offers him a break while still keeping his
attention.

9.   **Offer prizes for learning**. A star or an A+ written on
the top of a piece of paper has no meaning for an autistic
child. Autistic children look at the world in a very literal
sense. They see most things as black and white, and
have a hard time understanding "gray"—in other words,
things they can't touch, smell, see, taste, or hear. For
example, teaching about the wind, which is something

they can't see, is very difficult; but teaching about rain, which they can see falling and feel on their skin, is not.

As mentioned, stickers are always great rewards. Or, get a bunch of toys from a dollar store. Something your child can see and feel.

10. **Don't feel pressured by other parents boasting about what their child can do.** Many parents feel the need for one-upmanship in order to validate their abilities as the parent and teacher. Never make your child live up to anyone's expectations except yours: the realistic, achievable ones you set for him to accomplish during the school year. Each child, regardless of grade level or special needs, learns at his own pace.

TEACHING STYLE AND LEARNING STYLE

You'll also want to note how well your child attends to a lesson and how long his attention span is during each subject. Knowing this will help you tailor a curriculum and teaching style that he will be most responsive to for each subject.

Finally, note your child's learning style. Remember, not all lessons are learned sitting at a table in a classroom between the hours of 8:00 AM and 3:00 PM. Let your kids experience the world by exploring it. Some children learn better by doing rather than by reading. Take time to see how your child learns the best and introduce other ways of learning to help him. The purpose of taking notes at this stage is to help you decide how to begin teaching.

REEVALUATE YOUR PRIORITIES

Autistic children require a lot of one-on-one care. These children are a part of us, but they are trapped by their own minds, feeling lost, frustrated, and alone. It is up to *us* to find a way to connect with *them*, helping them be a part of our lives and a part of the family in which they live. To do this adequately, we must often make tough decisions and sacrifices, choosing to push aside those things that once seemed important, even if just temporarily.

These scenarios may sound familiar, for example: Choosing between having a spotless house or learning to deal with clutter and mess so that we can give our children the care they need. Choosing to miss parties or outings because we know that if we take our children, they will have meltdowns. Choosing to leave our children with babysitters or in daycares while we're at work. Choosing to quit our jobs or to cut back on our working hours to have more time to attend to our children. Many families whose insurance companies refuse to cover necessary autism treatments choose to pay for those services out of their own pockets or, if they can't afford it, take out loans; families have even gone into debt and lost their homes in order to cover such expenses.

These are not easy decisions, but the fact remains that families of autistic children are faced with these decisions on a daily basis, and having an autistic child often causes us to make sacrifices we may not have otherwise. As we evaluate our many options, our priorities tend to change as we see what's truly important in our lives.

MAKING THE CONNECTION

Every time you speak to your child, whether it is during a home-therapy or homeschooling session or while relaxing as a family at the end of the night, it is important to seek direct eye contact with him.

To do this, block out as much stimuli as possible. Place your faces very close together. As your child's eyes dart around, looking in other directions, use your hands or construction paper as blinders so the only thing he can see is your face. Don't stop until he has looked you in the eyes. Encourage him by saying, "Look in Mama's eyes with Billy's eyes." He needs to know where to look, how to look, what to look at, and with what he is looking. As with all other communication you have with him, at first, he will understand this instruction only when you use proper nouns. Once he begins to understand pronouns, however, you can change your messaging to him accordingly (saying "your eyes" instead of "Billy's eyes," and "my eyes" versus "Mama's eyes"). Depending on the severity of the autism, children gain such an understanding of pronouns at different rates, so the important thing is to tailor your language specifically to your child.

Another way to help your child connect with the world around him is to offer him toys to look at directly. Then, watching his eyes closely, be very specific about what you want him to do. For example, say, "Billy, look up at the red ball in your hands." When he looks, acknowledge it and praise him.

At first, the eye contact may just be for a split second, but that time will increase with positive encouragement.

Besides encouragement, another way you can teach your child to look at things is by pointing using *his* hand. Autistic children often see their hands and feet not as part of their bodies, but as separate and detached. As a result, some autistic children will use another person's hand as a tool, bringing it toward what they want. They do not point with their own hands because they have not made the connection that their hands are extensions of themselves.

To help your child point, start by standing behind him, extending his arm, and then holding his index finger out while curling the other fingers under into a fist. Point at a picture of something and name what is in the picture. With your free hand, you can gently turn his head so that he looks in the right direction. You can even gently tap his finger on the picture, repeating what he is looking at.

Start out with simple pictures that have little to distract your child from the main subject. If your child wants to use you as a tool by taking your hand and pointing at something else, take his hand to that object instead. For example, if your child takes your hand and points it to a book, instead take his hand helping him to point his finger at the book while asking "Read book?" keeping questions as simple as possible until he learns more communication skills.

Also, help your child gain body awareness by teaching him activities such as clapping and playing games like Where is Thumbkin? and This Little Piggy Went to Market, showing him how to hold his fingers up or how to wriggle certain toes. Allow him to use movement to learn, for example, have him jump on a trampoline to say the alphabet. Once your child learns body awareness, he will begin to communicate with others, which in turn, will encourage other skills to blossom.

DESENSITIZING YOUR CHILD

Sensory defensiveness can be a huge obstacle. Desensitizing is a must. Here are some suggestions for gently desensitizing your child.

Creating a play box of various textures is a good way to start. Be creative. Fill the box with different fabrics, such as silk, burlap, corduroy, or fur; objects such as corn cobs, pine cones, crumpled tinfoil, or a wig; substances like goop or shaving cream; and "instruments" such as clackers, noise makers, whistles, or a bike horn.

You can also let your child play in pudding and Jell-O with his hands, or eat spaghetti and smash peas with his fingers. By doing this, he learns not only about various textures but also about cause and effect—what happens when peas are smashed or Jell-O rolls out of his fingers.

Another idea: let your child taste the difference between foods that look the same or similar: salt and sugar, for instance, or chocolate syrup and maple syrup. In fact, just about anything in the kitchen can be turned into a sensory tool. Letting him clank pots and pans with a wooden or metal spoon teaches him to listen to the sounds he can make (cause and effect) and how the sound differs from one pot to another.

Brushing Therapy (Wilbarger Protocol) is a desensitization technique based on the theory of Sensory Integration. With this type of therapy, you use a soft plastic brush to rub your child's arms, legs, and back, but avoid the chest and stomach. *However, you should only use this technique—developed by Dr. Patricia Wilbarger, an occupational therapist and clinical psychologist—with proper instruction from a trained therapist.* Brushing Therapy can help your child develop needed motor and language skills, as well as appropriate social and emotional behavior.[20]

After receiving proper instruction and implementing the brushing therapy, along with joint compression, I modified this technique to make it more personal. After brushing, I would rub my son vigorously in a kind of rough massage, sometimes adding a scented lotion to stimulate other senses. Other times, I would have him lay on a blanket I intended to wash and apply such substances as lotion, facial scrubs, shaving cream, or baby oil to his arms, legs, and torso; the different textures and smells would elicit different reactions in him, not only stimulating his sense of touch but also his sense of smell and sight.

Another therapy is the Oral Tactile Technique (OTT), in which you massage the inside of your child's mouth. *Again, however, do not use this technique without first getting proper instruction.* With OTT, you use a clean, gloved hand to gently rub your child's gums, exploring his mouth with your index finger but being sure *NEVER* to stick your finger down the throat. A "normal" child undergoing such massage would move his tongue to touch your finger. However, children with limited speech do not develop the same kind of muscle control in the tongue that we take for granted; their limited speech gives them little opportunity to exercise those crucial muscles. For example, saying the word *Lion* requires the tongue first to curl upward, to make the *L* sound, and then to press against the roof of the mouth to make the *N* sound). An under stimulated mouth can cause your child's tongue to become limp, capable of very little movement or speech. After you implement

---

[20] Pediatric Building Blocks. "The Wilbarger Deep Pressure and Proprioceptive Technique (DPPT)." http://www. pbbkids.com.the_wilbarger_brushing_protocol.htm

the Oral Tactile Technique into your therapy sessions you may begin to see a change in your child. The muscles that your child's tongue needs to make speech have gained in strength and awareness: he will start to move his tongue to meet your finger.

This therapy also offers your child more awareness of his mouth, teaching him about the feel of the roof of his mouth, his teeth, the insides of his cheeks and lips, and under the tongue—parts that are all necessary to forming speech.

Finally, you may want to use a form of music therapy called Disc Ease. This therapy entails simply listening to a unique CD with headphones for up to thirty minutes a day for about two weeks. This music CD was specifically created for use in auditory-integration training. I have seen great results from this therapy when used in conjunction with a full sensory diet. To learn more about Disc Ease go to www.vison-audio.com.

REGULATION TOOLS

Regulation tools are tools or activities that your child can use to help calm down or to keep busy as you transition between lessons. Below are some basic regulation tools that you may want to have on hand. As you read through them, keep in mind that not all things need be bought new. If you are creative and crafty, you can make your own versions of these tools at a fraction of the retail cost.

> **A swing.** Hang a swing from the ceiling or buy a small hammock that's suspended on a metal frame. A hammock will hug your child's body, offering needed pressure or just a quiet place to relax. The Web site www.myhammock.com has a variety of swings for people with all types of disabilities. Choose a style that best fits your child's needs.

> **A trampoline.** You don't need a large trampoline, unless you have a large child, but a small trampoline that fits in the room is great. If you have a large enough room, an eight-foot trampoline only stands about eighteen inches off the floor and is great for both parent and child. Unless you have very high ceilings, though, the twelve-foot trampoline will stand too tall to keep indoors. An old mattress and box spring work well also.

"Pressure" tools. Large exercise balls to roll over the body to apply pressure feels great, and you can use them in your workouts too. You can also use pillows to apply pressure or just give great big bear hugs. Another idea is to make or purchase the weighted blankets or vests commonly used by therapists. A fishing vest with lots of pockets filled with dry beans works well. Or, you can sew extra pockets on a cheap coat that you have torn the sleeves off of. Or make your own vest using a pattern. Be creative and you can save yourself a lot of money.

A padded area. A loft or large counter that is padded can be great to climb on or jump off of into giant cushions or pillows. Providing an environment in which your child can climb and jump safely teaches gross motor skills, offers a different perspective of the environment, and provides overall body awareness.

A dark, quite place. Having quiet time is a great way for your child to escape from stimuli for a while. Because autistic children are easily overstimulated, having a special place that is theirs alone can be very useful in helping them regulate overwhelming feelings. A dark space filled with pillows and blankets, such as a pop-up tunnel or just a dark sheet hung in a corner of a room, makes a great play fort as well as a dark, quiet place in which your child can get away.

"Stimulus" tools. A ball pit or a bean table is great fun and also another sensory area. Rolling around in the ball pit offers pressure and stimulates tactile senses. A bean table does the same when you run your hands through the beans, and you can also use it as a learning tool, to teach things such as pouring and measuring.

COMMUNICATION IS KEY

It's time to learn a second language. Autism is a language all is its own, and sometimes your child's version may differ from that of other autistic children, so the trick is to understand his individual communication style.

Before you start using techniques to help your child communicate, there are some things you should understand. First, know that the better your child understands you, the better you will understand your child—so be sure to listen and watch.

It's also important to understand that your child will learn how to communicate his emotions by watching you. If you add that to the idea that not all communication is verbal, you'll begin to notice all of the little ways that we communicate to those around us every day: our facial expressions, body movements, and tones of voice, to name a few.

As mentioned, the first step to communicating with your child is to learn to listen and watch patiently. When you ask your child a question, give him at least thirty seconds to respond. If he does not understand what you are asking, learn to rephrase the question in a way that he may better understand it. As you listen, remember that the smallest sound from his mouth can be an attempt to communicate. In addition, learn to watch expressions and body movements; remember, not all communication is verbal.

One way to bolster communication for autistic children with limited speech capabilities is to use picture cards or PECs (Picture Exchange Communication System). Pointing to a picture of a book and saying the word "book," or making the sign for book when your child chooses the book card, will help encourage speech, identification, word recognition, and signing. Never stop talking, explaining things, and pointing.

You can also use exaggerated facial expressions to help your child learn about and eventually communicate his own emotions. Start by practicing your facial expressions in the mirror, so you can see what they look like and ensure that you are communicating your feelings appropriately. Then, add words to your expressions. When you are happy, show your child you are happy with an exaggerated face, and then tell him, using a happy tone of voice, "Daddy is very happy." Likewise, show your child when you are angry, but be sure to use a tone that associates to the angry face without yelling or screaming. A deep, slow voice is a good combination with the angry face. Also don't forget to let your child see you sad and don't be afraid to let him see you cry. Letting him know it's okay to cry and be sad will eventually help him to express these emotions too.

When you're ill, say, "Mommy has a tummy ache," while placing your hand on your stomach. Naming each body part or place you hurt will teach him how to communicate when he's not feeling well. Then, if you see him holding his hand on his forehead, you can ask, "Does Billy have a headache?"

Playing games makes learning communication fun for you and your child. Do mouth exercises together by rolling your tongue, puffing out your cheeks, making raspberries, chewing gum, and sucking on sour candy.

When teaching your child how to say specific words, enunciate very clearly, putting emphasis on the consonants. Remember to avoid gray areas; speak and think very literally, in terms of black and white, and be descriptive. Start with basic words you use all the time (come, more, go, sit, stop, yes, no). As your child learns these words, he can begin to communicate basic needs.

Using speech along with picture cards and hand gestures or sign language can also increase your child's communication skills. You are providing communication in the form of sound, sight, and movement. Simultaneously teaching your child three different forms of communication.

In time, your child can learn to communicate. Maybe at first with just pictures, however your child chooses to begin communicating with you will depend solely on them. And once you start to bridge the gap of communication, you will see your child blossom.

DIET

Some parents have seen great improvements in their children's autism symptoms by making dietary changes. The most common change is to the gluten-free/casin-free diet. Many parents have had great success with this diet in alleviating symptoms associated with autism. To learn more or to order gluten-free foods, go to www.glutenfreemall.com. In addition, many local grocery stores now carry some gluten-free foods. Organic and natural health-food stores sell them as well.

Another dietary change some parents make is to add vitamin and mineral supplements to their children's diets. Awaken Nutrition has multivitamin and mineral supplements specifically designed for a child with autism. Contact them at 1-800-267-5273 or www.awakennutrition.com.

Another item being added to the autistic child's diet is Threelac, a nutritional food supplement composed of live bacteria (learn more at www.NewLifeVitamins.com). This supplement may be helpful for children who have taken a lot of antibiotics, because antibiotics kill the bad bacteria in a person's system along with the good bacteria. Adding good bacteria into the diet through Threelac may help the immune system.

As an example of how beneficial a special diet can be, I am one of a very small group of people who were diagnosed with Phenylkentonuria (PKU) when babies began being tested for this disease in the late 1960s. As a result of this diagnosis, my brother and I were on the special PKU diet as children. Today we are among a very small group of those diagnosed with PKU who are now over the age of thirty-five and are perfectly normal. This is due both to the strict diet plan and the unwavering efforts of our parents who made sure we didn't go off the plan.

Regardless of the benefits, however, consistently maintaining a special diet for your child can be very difficult unless the entire family chooses to be on the diet as well, making inappropriate food choices for the autistic child less likely (since in that case, the only foods available in the family kitchen would be those included in the diet). However, not all special diets are beneficial for the whole family, but are good only for the child who needs them.

MEDICATION

Parents naturally struggle with the thought of putting their child on medication, wishing they could find other ways to help their child manage symptoms of autism. For those who have chosen to use medication, that decision was likely not made lightly.

Every child and every family situation is unique. Adding those family dynamics along with medical history to the equation of treating a child with medication makes "the best choice" different for every family. To get your individual family through this decision process, seek the help of medical professionals, who are most qualified to aide you in this decision.

Keep in mind that finding the right medication for your child may be a very long process, requiring you to try many medications. To ease this process, you will need to be patient and keep excellent records of your child's reactions to help your doctor know in which direction he needs to go next with the medication.

At the end of this book I have included an Appendix, which provides a couple simple forms you can use to organize and keep accurate records of the many doctors and therapists your child has seen along with a list of medications he has taken and any resulting reactions. Keeping detailed information will help not only your child's doctor, but also you, as a parent, and any other caretakers (for example, teachers and therapists) that your child may have.

One more important thing to remember through this process: be confident enough to question your doctor's findings, if they concern you. After all, doctors are only human and do make mistakes. In addition, treating autism sometimes requires a trial and error approach to see what works best in the end. If your doctor is not educated or up to date on the latest autism information, you can switch doctors or bring some literature with the latest findings to your appointment. Open-minded doctors will likely welcome this; they will know they can't possibly know everything there is to know in the changing world of autism. By helping to keep them up to date, you will help others as well as yourself.

BUILDING FRIENDSHIPS

A common fear of parents just beginning the homeschooling process is that their children will no longer have social interaction with peers or opportunities to build friendships. Many parents even fear that homeschooling will isolate children to the point that they will loose, or not obtain, the lifelong social skills needed to function in society.

Most people who feel this way have not been informed of or have not investigated the many opportunities available to homeschooled children. Many public school systems allow homeschooled children to participate in public school activities and events such as sports teams and clubs. In some communities homeschooling families gather in huge numbers, creating an environment in which children of all ages can meet and play with other homeschooled children.

Even for those of us with children who have difficulty developing friendships, there are many ways to help socialize our children. Doing something as simple as taking your child to town on a daily basis to learn how to interact with the many different people you meet will help. It is always possible to meet other families at church socials, county fairs, festivals, playgrounds, and malls. And even meeting kids in the doctor's office can give your child the opportunity to develop a friendship.

Remember, too, that your child doesn't need a dozen friends. Having one or two good friends that understand your child's special needs is wonderful, allowing him to develop close bonds without pressure from other kids to be a certain way or to do only popular things. He and his friend can learn to respect each other for who they are and not for what they do or what they have. Finally, be a good social role model and your children will learn by your example.

It wasn't easy for any of us growing up to try to develop friendships. At some point, each of us has been hurt or rejected by someone else. Part of growing up is learning to deal with disappointment. Likewise, some friendships may not work out for your child, but with your help, he can learn how to deal with the loss and disappointment and move on to new friendships.

Be supportive of your child, offering him guidance about relationships but allowing freedom enough for him to learn and explore.

REMEMBERING "YOU" TIME

When we become parents, our lives are flipped upside down with diaper changes, 2:00 AM feedings, and constant baby checkups. We are tired, worn, and looking forward to the days when our child sleeps through the night, is potty-trained, and can tell us he is hungry without crying.

When that time arrives, we can breathe a sigh of relief. But for some of us, that day never came. We never got a break from providing the constant one-on-one care that an infant requires. Our children need to be watched all the time, regardless of age, and we as parents have risen to the challenge.

But there comes a time when we realize that to consistently rise to that challenge, we have to also take care of ourselves. If you are burned out, you cannot be the best parent possible for your child.

However you choose to do it, however you find the time, you need to try to set aside part of every day just for you. Taking one evening a week or once a month is often not enough to refresh yourself. Here are some ideas: After your child goes to bed, read a book or watch a movie. During naptime, forget about the house and take a nap yourself. Or go surfing online. Or, take your time to call a friend, send e-mails, or just sit in the sun listening to the quiet. Whatever you choose to do, "you" time will be a great boost to your sanity and will lower your stress levels. It is your daily therapy.

Also, as a side note, remember to devote time to any other children in your life. Some siblings of autistic children feel neglected, forgotten, jealous, and angry. They need to feel special too. They need to be reminded that they are loved and cared for just as much as their sibling who requires so much of their parents' attention. Take some time for just you two,   making one day a week "his" day. On that day, he gets to choose what to do and with whom and where to go. Remember, everyone in the family is a part of autism—including siblings, grandparents, aunts and uncles, and even pets—not just the child who's been diagnosed.

Aggravation and Stress: Autism's Other Side Affects

Fortunately, public awareness of autism is growing. Unfortunately, that awareness comes by way of an increase in the incidences of autism. With one child in every one hundred fifty being diagnosed, the reality is that more and more people are either related to or know someone with this disorder. The result is growing public awareness not only about autism but about the obstacles it creates for affected families.

DEALING WITH THE UNINFORMED

Despite growing awareness about autism, the reality is that there are still many who do not know about or understand it. There will always be those who think they have all the answers and feel the need to give you their advice.

Have you ever had this experience: someone notices your child is autistic and then asks if he can do tricks? I was asked this very question by a cashier one day.

I looked at him and said, "My son is not a dog."

The cashier didn't seem discouraged, however, as he continued to ask rude, inappropriate questions.

"Well, can't he do things like Raymond in *Rainman*?" he asked.

"No!" I replied, "He is not a circus act or an idiot savant."

Granted, that was about six years ago, but even today, I am sometimes told by complete strangers that I need to discipline my son better, that I overindulge him, and that that's why he misbehaves. Such a comment seems to completely deny that autism is a legitimate disorder with genuine symptoms (such as outbursts in public). It also ignores the reality that there has yet to be one parent who has raised her child perfectly.

The fact is, making mistakes is a part of learning, even when that means learning to be a good parent. Just know you are doing your very best at the job of being a parent to your autistic child. Realize that parents of nonautistic children could not possibly understand the difficulties or know the harsh realities you face every day. And, finally, don't let their criticisms intimidate you. Be strong and confident in yourself.

Facing Contradicting Medical Information

How many times have you wondered, what caused this disorder in my child? What is it? Why can't it be stopped? Why can't they fix it? Was this my fault? Did I do something to cause my child to become autistic?

When children are diagnosed with autism for the first time, parents often play the blame game. It was my fault or it was yours. It happened because you did this or I did that.

If you've been the parent of an autistic child for long, though, you'll know that even the doctors and scientists who have spent years studying Autism Spectrum Disorder can't agree as to its cause. Some doctors have proof that Thimerosol, found in childhood vaccines, is a cause, while other physicians believe a genetic link or predisposition increases the risk of developing the disorder. Still others in the medical community believe that toxins in the environment are the reason.

There are medical facts to back up each theory, and yet autism is still listed as having an unknown cause, and no one effective treatment has been proven to work in all cases. Some swear by a change in diet, others believe intensive therapy works best, while still others promote an all-natural, organic lifestyle. The fact remains, however, that regardless of what caused autism in one child or what treatment worked best in another, the medical community has yet to agree on one specific cause or treatment.

So the best thing we can do as parents is to be objective. We must not be afraid to question a doctor's findings. We must look for alternative solutions, if the treatment norm doesn't fit our child's circumstances. We must realize that each family and child is different and unique, and as a result, we may not fit into a textbook description of autism. We must do what's best for our child and our family alone.

In addition, not every doctor is created equal. In a class of three hundred, not everyone graduated at the top, and those who graduated last are still doctors. So take what your doctor tells you as advice, not law, and don't be afraid to question the advice you are given. If you feel in your gut that something is wrong, say so.

I learned this the hard way. I stood meekly by as inept doctors and medical staff put my child through unnecessary distress, until I found my voice and took control of my son's health. Today, we have a wonderful team of doctors, physician assistants, and nurses who take extra special care of our son. They are truly a joy to know.

Understanding Autism and Divorce Statistics

Having a child with autism is very stressful on a family, and while some families grow closer because of it, others seem to break apart. If you have a split with your spouse, the important thing to remember is not to blame the child or the autism.

Consider that the divorce rate is over 50 percent for *all* married couples—regardless of whether their children (if they have any) are autistic or disabled in any way. For those of us who parent an autistic child and are married or in a committed relationship, we are just like everyone else—going through the trials of trying to maintain a healthy relationship with our significant other while raising a family.

In other words, if you have separated from your spouse, don't blame the autism; likely, the separation would have happened regardless. If you do attribute the break-up to family stress resulting from dealing with autism, do not share this with your child, as he might feel that you are blaming him or that you resent him for having special needs. It is common for any child (autistic or not) of a divorced parent to think he may be responsible for the divorce. Our autistic children are no different in that sense. Although it may seem that they are totally unaware of what is going on in their world, because of their lack of communication and eye contact, in reality, they are taking in their surroundings, including any negative thoughts, feelings, and conversations around them.

Be a positive role model for your child in the way you conduct yourself, and avoid exposing them to adult troubles and concerns. Children don't need to have adult worries invade their childhood; they have enough to deal with already.

Do You Know Where Your Child Is?

How many times have you heard on the news that the police are searching for a lost young child with autism or Down Syndrome, or even for an elderly person with Alzheimer's? For years, I have had trouble with my son walking out the door without my knowledge. Knowing he wasn't supposed to go outside without Mom or Dad, he would sneak out quietly, closing the locked door behind him. I've tried all sorts of things to keep him inside. I've put locks on the doors and he has learned how to unlock them. I've bolted the doors at the very top, so he couldn't reach the bolts; he would very quietly pull over a chair to stand on and unbolt the door. I was running out of ideas fast, and I constantly worried that he would leave and get lost or injured.

There is nothing scarier than suddenly realizing that your child who was standing next to you just one minute ago has disappeared, or going into his room thirty minutes after you put him down for a nap only to find an empty bed. You feel desperate to find him. You franticly look in all directions, calling his name. After you search the house thoroughly, you head outside to make a search of the grounds around your house. Your child is nowhere to be found, and you begin to panic.

If you haven't found yourself in this position already, you likely will sometime in the future. To help you minimize those chances, however, here are some ideas for ways to secure your home—and your child.

Security systems can offer some piece of mind. With these systems, alarms attached to your doors and windows can either alert you to an intruder coming in or to your child leaving the house, as they sound whenever the doors or windows open. To purchase such alarms for your home or for more information, go to http://www.doorandwindowalarm.com.

On the other hand, some security systems are very costly, and many families can't afford the additional expense. So here's an idea for an inexpensive but very effective "alarm" system that you can make on your own. I have had great success with hanging wind chimes from the ceiling in front of all the doors, so when a door was opened, it would make a terrible racket. As soon as I heard the wind chimes, I'd know right away that my son was trying to leave or take down the chimes so he could open the door.

An added benefit to using wind chimes was that, because he didn't like the sound they made when he came in contact with the door, eventually he just stopped trying to sneak out. Also, because I was able to catch him whenever he tried to leave, I started to use those instances as opportunities to teach him to ask to go out, encouraging him to use picture cards, speech, and sign language. Then I would reward him when he did ask by taking him out, even if it was at night or in the rain. He soon learned that it's not always fun to go outside. Sometimes it's cold and dark.

Having an alarm system only works when you are at home, however. I still worry when we are in public. What would I do if we were at the park or at a store, and my son wandered off without my knowing? What could I do to find him? **Project Lifesaver** is a public safety measure that is the most successful missing persons rescue program to date. Started in 1999 in Chesapeake, Virginia, it is now in forty-one states and parts of Canada. Through Project Lifesaver, a GPS tracking device can be placed in a bracelet that your child can wear, either on his wrist or ankle. This tracking system has been effective in 100 percent of the cases that it's been needed.[21] To find out more about Project Lifesaver and how to bring it to your neighborhood, go to http://www.projectlifesaver.org.

Or, here's a less expensive idea: Have you ever seen a parent walking along with a child and holding a kind of leash, which is attached to a harness that the child is wearing? Some have described this as walking your child, similar to walking a dog. I laughed the first time I saw this, but the idea is not new. My mother did the same thing with my little sister to keep her safe back in the 1970s. While this method of security has not always been socially acceptable, however, that doesn't make it any less effective. To a family who faces the many challenges of raising a child with autism, their child's safety is of the utmost importance.

---

[21] Project Lifesaver International. "Bringing Your Loved Ones Home." http://www.projectli fesaverinternational.com/aboutus.aspx

Taking Control of Your Child's Future

When my son was just eighteen months old, and my husband and I were new parents, we enjoyed our son's newfound smiles and words, and the little things he did that reminded us he was our little boy: the dark eyes and hair, and the stubborn temper of his father, his mom's pouty mouth and freckles. Our son was a part of us and we could see ourselves in him. We wanted him to have what we didn't, to be able to enjoy life, to be strong in character, to learn to be a good person without sacrificing who he was.

We had hopes for our son too. Maybe our burly little boy could go to school and play football, or maybe he'd be an A student. We hoped he'd pursue anything his little heart desired, and we knew that he'd be great at whatever he chose to do, whether that be following in his daddy's footsteps and becoming a farmer, supplying milk and beef for the country's grocery stores, or going his own way in a profession of his choosing. We'd fantasize about all the things that our little boy could grow up to be. In short, as all parents do, we wanted the best for him.

But then the day came when we knew something was wrong. At first, we didn't want to admit it to ourselves, but when we got the diagnosis, we knew our dreams were gone. We could no longer see our little boy growing up to be anything. We could no longer see what the future might hold. In fact, we could no longer see past the next tantrum. Our dreams became stagnant.

In addition, we felt that somehow, in some way, we had failed as parents. It was our job as parents to keep our child safe from sickness and injury, and we had failed to keep him from autism. We also felt lost and alone, as though we were the only parents in the world going through this ordeal with their child. Although we had the support of our extended family, you know as well as I do that at least sometimes, even with all the support in the world, no one can truly understand what it is to have this happen to your child. No one can truly share the heartache you feel every day when you look into that little face and wish you knew how to stop the suffering and confusion, the knowledge that your child wants so much to be a part of your life but just doesn't know how to tell you. Here is a poem I wrote that somewhat describes the heartache I felt and that I still feel from time to time:

HIDDEN HOLLOW

Trapped in a world he alone knows. Lost and confused, escape is forbidden. A prism of reflection hidden deep behind dull, flat eyes void of life, of body, of spirit, yearning to be who you are and not what he is, for no one can truly understand his pain. He stays in the shadows where he hides away from society, who keeps him locked in his blackness, shunned by wondering, probing eyes and spiteful tongues. Although the embarrassment is theirs, unwilling to understand his pain, refusing to try, alone he remains.

Deep within this sticky tar, a light shines, searching, illuminating, making the forbidden escape plausible, even possible, so he may break free from his captivity, guiding, stumbling footsteps, as he climbs out of his great precipice only to loose his grip on the next rung, falling back three. The constant struggle to reach out for the light overwhelms.

Slowly understanding, grasping at hope as sparks ignite, cognitive ability lost and forgotten. For a moment, perhaps just a flicker, he looks deep into your heart to say, "I'm trapped! Help me escape this torture." Unable to articulate, rocking and repetitive moans are his cries of desperation.

After a while, though, we learned how to cope with the autism and accept it for what it was. We decided that to help our son, we needed to take control of the situation the best we could rather than playing the part of the victim, letting the disorder control our lives and our son's future. When we did that, the hopelessness and guilt started to fade. Our priorities changed from more superficial things, such as whether our son would become a doctor or lawyer, to those things in life that are *really* important.

We now look at life more realistically. We realize our son may not be the next Bill Gates or Brett Favre, and we are alright with that. Through hard work, however, we can still have hope that he will grow up to be happy and healthy, to be a productive member of society, and to feel he has a purpose in this world. And we have no doubt that he will always be a joy in our lives.

Whatever end of the spectrum your child is on, whatever dreams that diagnosis of autism has dashed, you still have hope. As parents of autistic children, we must keep hope alive by trying with every fiber of our beings to break down that wall of autism and reach the person hiding inside. Until nothing is left to be done, we must try every day to break into their world to become a part of it, and by doing so, maybe we can pull them back into ours.

Right from the start, we must take control of our children's futures. We must be their voices, speaking out and advocating for them.

Our children need someone to protect their rights when words or social awareness fail them because, unfortunately, there are still people in this world who don't care that your child is disabled. They don't care that he doesn't understand when he has offended someone. They don't care *why* your child is screaming in the middle of the store; they just want you to shut him up. In this "me" society, more and more people have become concerned with themselves at the expense of the persons next to them. Anyplace you go in this world, you will find people intolerant of others who are different. Of course, that doesn't mean we should reply in kind—we want to be above that level of behavior and, in turn, become tolerant of them. In the process, however, we can try to educate them, even if just a little.

And as mentioned, we must have adequate communication with those involved in our children's care in order to be able to speak out for them— remember the notebook idea mentioned earlier.

In short, as you sit quietly today reading the last of this book, do not feel overwhelmed and discouraged. Your child has you, and as a parent, you are a powerful force to be reckoned with. The love and devotion you have for your child shows through your willingness to help. And that willingness will pay off. Slowly, day by day, month by month, you will see progress, and that progress will give you more hope. Then someday, you will look back and ask yourself, "How did I do it? How did I manage?" But you will.

When that day comes, look yourself in the mirror and smile, for you are the one who made it happen. You are the one who made sacrifices and spent hours upon hours learning and teaching and giving and just loving your child. By your force, determination, and plain willpower you made a difference.

Be strong and be brave, knowing you are doing the very best job you can in a very difficult situation. You have the power to make a difference in the life of your child.

About the Author

Kathleen Mueller spent most of her childhood in a small town in Wisconsin, learning the values and experiencing the benefits of small-town living. She earned an associate's degree in photography and, after college, became a certified nursing assistant, caring for the elderly as well as for disabled children. That later experience gave her an advantage when the day came to care for an autistic child.

The challenge of mothering a child with autism hasn't changed Kathleen's personal dreams. She has published poems through the National Library of Poetry, earning two Editor's Choice Awards for her work. She also owns a company called Creative Artistry, in which she creates DVDs, compiling people's visual images with nostalgic songs and artwork to create an action-packed walk down memory lane.

Kathleen and her husband of fourteen years raise their son on a farm. Her life is busy, but she enjoys the challenges life throws. The struggles we face and obstacles we overcome only make us stronger.

If you wish to share your stories with Kathleen, ask questions, or just need to talk, please feel free to contact her at kathleenmueller2008@yahoo.com.

Appendix: Medical Charts

DOCTORS & SPECIALISTS

Doctor	Specialty	Clinic	Number

Doctor	Specialty	Clinic	Number

Doctor	Specialty	Clinic	Number

Doctor	Specialty	Clinic	Number

MEDICATION HISTORY

Medication:_____ Date:_____

Doctor: _____

Clinic:_____

Number:_____

Reason
Prescribed:_____

_____

_____

Reaction
Positive/Negative:_____

_____

_____

Medication:_____ Date:_____

Doctor: _____

Clinic:_____

Number:_____

Reason
Prescribed:_____

_____

_____

Reaction
Positive/Negative:_____

_____

_____

Medication:_____ Date:_____

Doctor: _____

Clinic:_____

Number:_____

Reason
Prescribed:_____

_____

_____

Reaction
Positive/Negative:_____

_____

_____

MEDICATION HISTORY

Medication:_____ Date:_____
Doctor: _____
Clinic:_____
Number:_____
Reason
Prescribed:_____
_____
_____

Reaction
Positive/Negative:_____
_____
_____

Medication:_____ Date:_____
Doctor: _____
Clinic:_____
Number:_____
Reason
Prescribed:_____
_____
_____

Reaction
Positive/Negative:_____
_____
_____

Medication:_____ Date:_____
Doctor: _____
Clinic:_____
Number:_____
Reason
Prescribed:_____
_____
_____

Reaction
Positive/Negative:_____
_____
_____

MEDICATION HISTORY

Medication:_____ Date:_____

Doctor: _____

Clinic:_____

Number:_____

Reason
Prescribed:_____

_____

_____

Reaction
Positive/Negative:_____

_____

_____

Medication:_____ Date:_____

Doctor: _____

Clinic:_____

Number:_____

Reason
Prescribed:_____

_____

_____

Reaction
Positive/Negative:_____

_____

_____

Medication:_____ Date:_____

Doctor: _____

Clinic:_____

Number:_____

Reason
Prescribed:_____

_____

_____

Reaction
Positive/Negative:_____

_____

_____

MEDICATION HISTORY

Medication:_____ Date:_____

Doctor: _____

Clinic:_____

Number:_____

Reason

Prescribed:_____

_____

_____

Reaction

Positive/Negative:_____

_____

_____

Medication:_____ Date:_____

Doctor: _____

Clinic:_____

Number:_____

Reason

Prescribed:_____

_____

_____

Reaction

Positive/Negative:_____

_____

_____

Medication:_____ Date:_____

Doctor: _____

Clinic:_____

Number:_____

Reason

Prescribed:_____

_____

_____

Reaction

Positive/Negative:_____

_____

_____

MEDICATION HISTORY

Medication:_____ Date:_____

Doctor: _____

Clinic:_____

Number:_____

Reason
Prescribed:_____

_____

_____

Reaction
Positive/Negative:_____

_____

_____

Medication:_____ Date:_____

Doctor: _____

Clinic:_____

Number:_____

Reason
Prescribed:_____

_____

_____

Reaction
Positive/Negative:_____

_____

_____

Medication:_____ Date:_____

Doctor: _____

Clinic:_____

Number:_____

Reason
Prescribed:_____

_____

_____

Reaction
Positive/Negative:_____

_____

_____

MEDICATION HISTORY

Medication:_____ Date:_____

Doctor: _____

Clinic:_____

Number:_____

Reason
Prescribed:_____

_____

_____

Reaction
Positive/Negative:_____

_____

_____

Medication:_____ Date:_____

Doctor: _____

Clinic:_____

Number:_____

Reason
Prescribed:_____

_____

_____

Reaction
Positive/Negative:_____

_____

_____

Medication:_____ Date:_____

Doctor: _____

Clinic:_____

Number:_____

Reason
Prescribed:_____

_____

_____

Reaction
Positive/Negative:_____

_____

_____

Daily Medication Schedule

Medication	Dosage	Time Given	Date

Medication	Dosage	Time Given	Date

Medication	Dosage	Time Given	Date

Medication	Dosage	Time Given	Date

Medication	Dosage	Time Given	Date

Medication	Dosage	Time Given	Date

Medication	Dosage	Time Given	Date

Medication	Dosage	Time Given	Date

Glossary

Attention Deficit Hyperactivity Disorder (ADHD) Disorder characterized by prominent symptoms of inattention and/or hyperactivity-impulsivity.

Autism Spectrum Disorder (ASD) Developmental disability that comes from a neurological disorder affecting the brain. It is characterized by the abnormal development of communication skills.

Bipolar I Disorder Disorder characterized by one or more manic or mixed episodes, usually accompanied by major depressive episodes.

Bipolar II Disorder Disorder characterized by one or more major depressive episodes accompanied by at least one hypomanic episode.

Casin-Free Diet Diet free of all foods, drinks, and medications containing milk or milk byproducts.

Gluten-Free Diet Diet free of all foods, drinks, and medications made with gluten.

Major Depressive Disorder Disorder characterized by one or more major depressive episodes with at least two weeks of depressed mood or loss of interest accompanied by at least four additional symptoms of depression.

Occupational Therapy (OT) Holistic, patient-centered, occupation-based approach to life- skills development.

Obsessive Compulsive Disorder (OCD) Disorder characterized by recurrent obsessions or compulsions severe enough to be time-consuming or cause marked distress or significant impairment.

Pervasive Developmental Disorder (PDD) Disorder characterized by severe deficits and pervasive impairment in multiple areas of development.

Physical Therapy (PT) Services to restore function, improve mobility, relieve pain, and prevent or limit permanent physical disabilities.

Project Lifesaver Project in which a GPS tracking device is placed in a bracelet to find lost persons.

Rett Syndrome Disorder of the nervous system that leads to development reversals; most commonly seen in areas of expressive language and hand use.

[22] WebMD. Autism Health Center, "Understanding Autism—the Basics" and "What Is Autism?" http://www.webmd.com/brain/autism/understanding-autism-basics

Resources

Over the years I have found many Web sites, books, programs, and therapies that can help in raising your autistic child. Some of the information in these resources worked well for us, while some didn't work at all, so as you do research, remember to take only the information that's best for your situation. Also know that the most important piece of information I learned in all my research is that is not all media is beneficial, but not all of it harmful either. I needed to sift through the good and the bad to find what worked for me and my family.

WEB SITES

The following Web sites offer information about raising a child with autism or special needs:

http://www.nytimes.com

http://www.unification.net

http://www.jesusjournal.com

http://www.babybumblebee.com

http://www.familiywatchdog.com

http://www.topics-ent.com

http://www.seedsofdeception.com

The following sites offer information about alternative foods and allergies:

http://www.foodallergytest.com

http://www.amazon.com

http://www.organicconsumers.org

http://www.iansnaturalfoods.com

http://www.123candida.com

The following sites might offer answers to your homeschooling or learning questions:

http://www.K12.com

http://www.local.com

http://www.CafeMom.com

http://www.school-your-way.com

http://www.home-ed-magazine.com

BOOKS

The following may help you learn more about homeschooling or creating your own therapy:

- *American SIGN Language Dictionary*, by Martin L. A. Sternberg

- *Signing How to Speak with Your Hands*, by Elaine Costello

- *Homeschooling the Early Years: Your Complete Guide to Successfully Homeschooling the 3- to 8-Year Old Child*, by Linda Dobson

- *Homeschooling the Teen Years: Your Complete Guide to Successfully Homeschooling the 13- to 18-Year Old*, by Cafi Cohen and Janie Levine Hellyer

- *Homeschooling the Child with ADD (or Other Special Needs): Your Complete Guide to Successfully Homeschooling the Child with Learning Differences,* by Lenore Colacion Hayes

- *Homeschooling the Child with Asperger's Syndrome: Real Help for Parents Anywhere and on Any Budget,* by Lise Pyles

- *Homeschooler's Guide to FREE Teaching Aids*, Educator's Progress Service, Inc.

- *Homeschooling ALMANAC*, by Mary and Michael Leppert

- *The Homeschooling BOOK OF ANSWERS*, by Linda Dobson

If you homeschool or plan to, you may be able to use the following publications as textbooks:

- Eyewitness Books
- *Preschool Ultimate Skill Builder*, Learning Horizons
- *The Complete Book of Presidents & States Grades 4–6*, McGraw-Hill Children's Publishing
- *The Complete Book of United States History Grades 3–5*, McGraw-Hill Children's Publishing
- *The Grapes of Math*, by Greg Tang
- *Mighty Machines*, by Adam Hibbert, Chirs Oxlade, and James Pickering
- *Questions and Answers: INVENTIONS: How? Why? Where? When?*, by Louise Spilsbury
- *World History Encyclopedia*, Parragon Books, Ltd.
- World of Science, Parragon Books, Ltd.
- *Earth and Space*, by Anita Ganeri, John Malam, Clare Oliver, Adam Hibbert (Parragon Books)

The following books offer information and support to caretakers of children with special needs:

- *A Special Kind of Love: For Those Who Love Children with Special Needs*, by Susan Titus Osborn and Janet Lynn Mitchell
- *Raising a Sensory Smart Child: The Definitive Handbook for Helping Your Child with Sensory Integration Issues*, by Lindsey Biel and Nancy Peske
- *The Ups and Downs of Raising a Bipolar Child: A Survival Guide for Parents*, by Judith Lederman and Candida Fink
- *Treating Huckleberry Finn: A New Narrative Approach to Working with Kids Diagnosed ADD/ADHA*, by David Nylund
- *Emergency Medical Treatment*, by Stephen Vogel, MD and David Manhoff
- *Learning Disabilities from a Parent's Perspective: What You Need to Know to Understand, Help, & Advocate for Your Child*, by Kim E. Glenchur
- *Ten Things Every Child Wishes to Know*, by Ellen Notbohm
- *Ten Things Your Student with Autism Wished You Knew*, by Ellen Notbohm and Veronica Zysk
- *Autism and the God Connection*, by William Stillman

Videos and Television Shows

Schoolhouse Rock

The 100 Greatest Discoveries, the Discovery Channel

"Mount St. Helens–Explosive Evidence for Catastrophe," by the Institute for Creation Research

"Inside the Living Body," by National Geographic

"The Human Body: Major Systems and Organs," Goldhil Entertainment

"The Human Body: Nervous System," Goldhil Entertainment

"The Human Body: Musculoskeletal System," Goldhil Entertainment

Bill Nye the Science Guy, PBS

Check *TV Guide* for upcoming episodes that you can sit and watch as a family

Television Channels

Animal Planet

The Discovery Channel

The History Channel

Interactive and Hands-on Learning Toys

Around the World, by Scientific Toys, Ltd.

Planetarium, by Scientific Toys, Ltd.

Flip for Phonics, by V-Tech

LeapPad Learning System, by Leap Frog

Etch-a-Sketch, by Fisher Price

Foam Numbers and Letter Puzzles (several companies make these)

Interactive Globes (several companies make these)

Flash Cards (these come in several different kinds—letter sounds, phonics, addition, subtraction, and more—and are made by different companies)

Bibliography

1. Autism and Pdd Support Network: What is Autism? The History of Autism.

2. Autism Society of America: History

3. Autism and Pdd Support Network: What is Autism? Autism Definition from Columbia Encyclopedia.

4. Autism and Pdd Support Network: What is Autism? Autism Symptoms.

5. Autism and Pdd Support Network: What is Autism? Autism Symptom Checklist.

6. Wisconsin State Journal: Genes Linked to Autism Found, By Carrie Peyton Dahlberg, The Sacramento Bee. 1/26/2008 A3

7. Autism and Pdd Support Network: What is Autism? What Causes Autism?

8. Centers for Disease Control and Prevention. CDC. Vaccine Safety, "Mercury and Vaccines (Thimerosol)"

9. Autism and Pdd Support Network: Diagnosing Autism.

10. Autism and Pdd Support Network: Diagnosing Autism, Baby's Communication Milestones.

11. Autism and Pdd Support Network: Diagnosing Autism, DSM-IV Criteria.

12. Autism and Pdd Support Network: What is Autism? Autism Symptoms Checklist.

13. Biomedical Treatments for Autism: "About the Autism Research and the DAN! Protocol." By Lisa Jo Rudy.

14. Manataka American Indian Council: Native Remedies, Autism Remedy, Autism-Proven Natural Treatment for Autistic Children, Teens, and Adults.

15. Autism Research Unit-Secretin as an intervention for autism: The Use of Secretin for the treatment of Autism.

16. Autism Treatments: CranioSacral Therapy (CST) for Autistic Children.

17. Treatments for Autism: Hyperbaric Oxygen Treatment, Hyperbaric Oxygen Treatment Study.

18. Autism Treatments: Live Cell & Stem Cell Therapy, Live Cell Therapy, Stem Cell Therapy.

19. Autism Treatments: Anti-Fungal Treatment.

20. Pediatric Building Blocks: The Wilbarger Deep Pressure and Proprioceptive Technique (DPPT).

21. Pediatric Building Blocks: The Wilbarger Deep Pressure and Proprioceptive Technique (DPPT).

22. EAse(Electronic Auditory Stimulation Effect): Sound Sensitive

23. Project Lifesaver International: "Bringing Your Loved Ones Home"

24. WebMD: Better Information Better Health, Autism Health Center, Understanding Autism- the Basics.